48 Powerful Meal Recipes That Will Help Control Your High Blood Pressure:

A Natural Solution to Hypertension without Pills or Medicine

By

Joe Correa CSN

COPYRIGHT

© 2016 Live Stronger Faster Inc.

All rights reserved

Reproduction or translation of any part of this work beyond that permitted by section 107 or 108 of the 1976 United States Copyright Act without the permission of the copyright owner is unlawful.

This publication is designed to provide accurate and authoritative information in regard to the subject matter covered. It is sold with the understanding that neither the author nor the publisher is engaged in rendering medical advice. If medical advice or assistance is needed, consult with a doctor. This book is considered a guide and should not be used in any way detrimental to your health. Consult with a physician before starting this nutritional plan to make sure it's right for you.

ACKNOWLEDGEMENTS

This book is dedicated to my friends and family that have had mild or serious illnesses so that you may find a solution and make the necessary changes in your life.

48 Powerful Meal Recipes That Will Help Control Your High Blood Pressure:

A Natural Solution to Hypertension without Pills or Medicine

By

Joe Correa CSN

CONTENTS

Copyright

Acknowledgements

About The Author

Introduction

48 Powerful Meal Recipes That Will Help Control Your High Blood Pressure: A Natural Solution to Hypertension without Pills or Medicine

Additional Titles from This Author

ABOUT THE AUTHOR

After years of Research, I honestly believe in the positive effects that proper nutrition can have over the body and mind. My knowledge and experience has helped me live healthier throughout the years and which I have shared with family and friends. The more you know about eating and drinking healthier, the sooner you will want to change your life and eating habits.

Nutrition is a key part in the process of being healthy and living longer so get started today. The first step is the most important and the most significant.

INTRODUCTION

Hypertension or high blood pressure, which many specialists call "the silent killer" is a very commonly spread condition. It may not be initially noticeable for a very long time but long term it leads to kidney disease, heart attacks, strokes, etc. Not to worry, this condition is very easily preventable and curable, in fact, it's all in your own hands and it's all about your diet. Recipes featured in this book consist of scientifically proven ingredients to lower your blood pressure like: beans, broccoli, buckwheat, red peppers, low fat dairy and, generally speaking, foods rich in calcium, potassium and magnesium. While your main might be to lower or prevent high blood pressure, some additional benefits of incorporating these low fat recipes into your diet may be: weight loss, digestive health improvement, and a major energy and positivity boost. This book presents all kinds of recipes with a variety of ingredients such as: vegetables, fruits, low fat dairy, nuts, grains and spices. These recipes do not contain salt or sugar but perfectly compensate for it with spices and all kinds of natural sweeteners like honey. Needless to say, this book will serve you as a guiding star, leading you to your ideal weight, while achieving health and lowered blood pressure.

48 POWERFUL MEAL RECIPES THAT WILL HELP CONTROL YOUR HIGH BLOOD PRESSURE: A NATURAL SOLUTION TO HYPERTENSION WITHOUT PILLS OR MEDICINE

1. Oat bran muffins with raisins and walnuts

Benefits: Using high in fiber oat bran as flour substitution makes this recipe especially suitable to lower blood pressure and improve digestive health. Raisins, provided they are made from organic grapes, are not only rich in potassium but also provide a rich sweet flavor of this healthy breakfast option.

Ingredients:

- 180 g oat bran
- 30 ml low fat milk
- 1 egg
- 4 tbsp honey
- 2 tbsp coconut oil (optional)
- 0,5 tsp baking powder
- 30 g raisins
- 30 g walnuts

How to prepare:

Whisk together an egg, honey, milk and melted coconut oil. Incorporate oat bran and baking powder. Pour the mixture into individual paper muffin baking cups. Bake for 15 minutes at 425 F until golden brown. Makes 7 muffins.

Per serving: 182 calories, sodium 116 mg, potassium 114 mg, sugars 7 g

2. Oat bran banana pancakes

Benefits: Banana and oat bran are both amazing sources of potassium. Banana and low-fat yogurt base of this delicious breakfast pancakes help lose weight, lower blood pressure and boost energetic levels for the rest of the day.

Ingredients:

- 100 g oat bran
- 1 ripe banana
- 80 g plain low fat yogurt
- 2 tbsp. honey
- baking powder

How to prepare: Mush the banana and combine it with low fat yogurt and honey, incorporate oat bran and baking powder. Pour about 2 tablespoons per pancake onto a pan and fry in coconut or olive oil until crispy on both sides. Makes about 8 pancakes.

Per serving: 66 calories, sodium 58 mg, potassium 97 mg, sugars 6 g

3. Warm oatmeal with prunes and mixed nuts

Benefits: Prunes have always been considered one of the best digestive remedies. They are also a good source of potassium and variety of minerals. Nuts are packed with protein, fiber and essential fats.

Ingredients:

- 100 g oats
- 150 ml low fat milk
- 50 g diced dried prunes
- 40 g chopped walnuts, pistachios, hazelnuts etc.

How to prepare: Bring milk to a simmer in a saucepan, add diced prunes and oats, simmer for 8 minutes on low heat while stirring. Top with cinnamon and chopped nuts. Makes 3 servings.

Per serving: 270 calories, sodium 25 mg, potassium 390 mg, sugars 9 g

4. "Baklava" diet breakfast

Benefits: Tangerines are packed with flavonoids, vitamin C, vitamin A, folate and potassium. Low fat yogurt is an awesome source of calcium, vitamin B-2, vitamin B-12, potassium, and magnesium.

Ingredients:

- 150 g low fat Greek yogurt
- 1 tbsp honey
- 20 g pistachios
- 10 g almonds
- 1 small tangerine

How to prepare: Chop pistachios and almonds, add diced tangerine. Pour Greek yogurt and honey over the mixture and mix thoroughly. Makes 2 servings.

Per serving: 114 calories, sodium 162 mg, potassium 157 mg, sugars 5 g

5. Oatmeal with pecans, plums and honey

Benefits: Pecans are high in healthy unsaturated fat and contain more than 19 vitamins and minerals including vitamins A, B, and E, folic acid, calcium, magnesium, phosphorus, potassium, and zinc. **Plums will satisfy your hunger for a very long time.**

Ingredients:

- 100 g oats
- 150 ml low fat milk
- 20 g chopped pecans
- 2 plums
- 2 tbsp honey

How to prepare: Bring milk to a simmer in a saucepan, add oats simmer for 8 minutes on low heat while stirring. Top with chopped pecans and diced plums. Finish with a drizzle of honey. Makes 3 servings.

Per serving: 230 calories, sodium 25 mg, potassium 233 mg, sugars 9 g

6. Exotic raw buckwheat breakfast porridge

Benefits: Buckwheat is a super-food that is excellent for digestion and blood pressure. It is one of the best sources of high-quality, easily digestible protein. Kiwis are considered one of the best fruits to lower blood pressure.

Ingredients:

- 200 g raw buckwheat
- 200 ml water
- 150 ml low fat milk
- 1 kiwi
- 30 g melon

How to prepare: Leave buckwheat covered in water overnights to soak. Drain the water and put buckwheat, milk, diced kiwi and melon to a blender and mix well. Makes 4 servings.

Per serving: 220 calories, sodium 23 mg, potassium 319 mg, sugars 3.5 g

7. Summer berries yogurt bowl

Benefits: Strawberries, blueberries and raspberries are rich in nutrients, antioxidants and phytochemicals which may help prevent and reverse diabetes, high blood pressure and even certain types of cancer.

Ingredients:

- 200 g low fat yogurt
- 50 g fresh blueberries
- 50 g fresh strawberries
- 50 g fresh raspberries
- 50 g oats

How to prepare: Combine berries, yogurt and oats together in a bowl and serve. Makes 3 servings.

Per serving: 90 calories, sodium 48 mg, potassium 280 mg, sugars 7 g

8. Plum and nectarine smoothie

Ingredients: Nectarines are very rich in beta-carotene, vitamin A, vitamin C, fiber and potassium. Plums contain no saturated fats and are full of minerals and vitamins.

Ingredients:

- 100 g low fat yogurt
- 150 ml low fat milk
- 4 medium ripe plums
- 1 nectarine

How to prepare: Put yogurt, milk, diced peeled plums and nectarine and mix fell. Pour into glasses and serve. Makes 2 servings.

Per serving: 99 calories, sodium 69 mg, potassium 376 mg, sugars 12 g

9. Creamy buckwheat

Benefits: This recipe possesses all the benefits of super-foods like buckwheat and banana. Low fat milk makes it especially diet-friendly and healthy.

Ingredients:

- 100 g buckwheat
- 200 ml water
- 40 ml low fat milk
- 1 banana
- 2 tbsp honey

How to prepare: Bring water to a boil in a saucepan, add buckwheat and simmer for 10 minutes or until it soaks all the liquid. Add diced bananas and drizzle with honey. Makes 4 servings.

Per serving: 157 calories, sodium 20 mg, potassium 218 mg, sugars 9 g

10. Baked apples with oats and nuts

Benefits: Apples are extremely rich in important antioxidants, flavanoids, and dietary fiber, they may help reduce the risk of developing cancer, hypertension, diabetes, and heart disease.

Ingredients:

- 2 medium apples
- 3 tbsp honey
- 40 g oats
- 30 g walnuts or pecans

How to prepare: Peel apples and cut them in half, remove the hull and place apples onto a baking tray lined with parchment paper. Chop walnuts or pecans, mix them with oats and top apples with the mixture. Drizzle honey on top and place in a preheated oven at 370 F for 20 minutes or until apples are tender and golden. Makes 4 servings.

Per serving: 179 calories, sodium 2 mg, potassium 181 mg, sugars 4 g

11. Breakfast quinoa salad with baked peaches and nuts

Benefits: Quinoa contains iron, magnesium, potassium, calcium, vitamin E, and fiber. Peaches offer a rich variety of calcium, potassium, magnesium.

Ingredients:

- 50 g quinoa
- 150 ml water
- 40 ml low fat milk
- 2 medium peaches
- 40 g pistachios

How to prepare: Chop the peaches, place them onto a cooking tray, drizzle with honey and bake at 400 F for about 25 minutes. Meanwhile cook your quinoa as stated on the packaging. Combine chopped pistachios, peaches and quinoa, pour in room temperature milk and serve warm. Makes 3 servings.

Per serving: 164 calories, sodium 80 mg, potassium 377 mg, sugars 6 g

12. Light panna cotta with apricots honey and walnuts

Benefits: This low fat creamy and delicate dessert may become one of your favorites. Apricots provide you with fiber, potassium, iron, and antioxidants.

Ingredients:

- 200 g low fat yogurt
- 100 ml low fat milk
- vanilla extract
- gelatin or agar
- 1 tbsp honey
- 2 small apricots
- 30 g walnuts

How to prepare: Cover gelatin or agar with water and leave it to soak for 10 minutes, meanwhile heat your milk and yogurt in a saucepan while stirring in order to prevent any lumps. Add 1 tbsp honey for sweetness. Dice your apricots, combine with chopped walnuts and evenly distribute the mixture between 3 little baking forms. Incorporate gelatin or agar into the liquid and pour into the forms. Leave them in a freezer for at least 6 hours.

Sprinkle with chopped walnuts and drizzle with honey (optional). Makes 3 servings.

Per serving: 156 calories, sodium 63 mg, potassium 324 mg, sugars 10 g

13. Blueberries, plum and hazelnut salad

Benefits: This recipe possesses all the benefits of plums and blueberries, as well as hazelnuts. Hazelnuts are rich in unsaturated fats, high in magnesium, calcium and vitamins B and E.

Ingredients:

- 150 g blueberries
- 4 medium plums
- 40 g hazelnuts
- leafy greens of your choice

How to prepare: Dice your plums and chop your hazelnuts. Combine all the ingredients together in a salad bowl and serve. Makes 2 servings.

Per serving: 139 calories, sodium 0 mg, potassium 221 mg, sugars 5 g

14. Baked pumpkin and carrot salad

Benefits: Pumpkin helps you to lower blood pressure and is extremely beneficial for your heart. Carrots are rich in vitamin A, Vitamin C, Vitamin K, vitamin B8, pantothenic acid, folate, potassium, iron, copper, and manganese.

Ingredients:

- 200 g pumpkin
- 100 g carrot
- 100 g feta cheese
- 1 tbsp honey
- 30 g pine nuts

How to prepare: Dice your pumpkin and carrots, drizzle with honey and bake until tender at 400 F. Cut feta cheese into small cubes. Combine all the ingredients together and serve. Makes 3 servings.

Per serving: 139 calories, sodium 0 mg, potassium 221 mg, sugars 5 g

15. Cherry tomato pomegranate salad

Benefits: Cherry tomatoes are a good source of vitamins and minerals essential for good health. Pomegranates are proven to have blood pressure-reducing properties.

Ingredients:

- 150 g cherry tomatoes
- 1 medium pomegranate
- 1 medium red onion
- 50 g feta cheese

How to prepare:

Cut cherry tomatoes in half, roughly chop the onion and feta cheese and combine with the pomegranate. Drizzle with lemon juice (optional) and serve. Makes 3 servings.

Per serving: 101 calories, sodium 190 mg, potassium 316 mg, sugars 10 g

16. Green salad with creamy avocado sauce

Benefits: Broccoli is a very good source of dietary fiber, vitamin B6, vitamin E, manganese, vitamin B1, vitamin A , potassium and calcium. Incredibly nutricious and packed with potassium and other minerals avocado is essential to have in your diet.

Ingredients:

- 100 g broccoli
- 100 g green peas
- spinach (to taste)
- 0.5 ripe avocado
- 50 g low fat yogurt

How to prepare: Boil your broccoli for 15 minutes and chop them. Combine with peas and fresh spinach leaves. Put avocado pulp and yogurt in a blender and mix thoroughly. Pour the sauce on top of the salad and drizzle with lemon juice or olive oil (optional). Makes 2 servings.

Per serving: 184 calories, sodium 59 mg, potassium 722 mg, sugars 5 g

17. Sweet potato patties with spinach and mushrooms

Benefits: Sweet potatoes are an excellent source of vitamin A, vitamin C, manganese, copper, pantothenic acid and potassium. Spinach is packed with protein, fiber, vitamins A, C, E and K, thiamin, vitamin B6, calcium, iron, magnesium, phosphorus, potassium.

Ingredients:

- 100 g sweet potato
- Spinach
- 100 g mushrooms
- 1 small red onion
- Olive oil
- 60 g buckwheat flour

How to prepare: Chop the onion finely and fry in olive oil until slightly brown. Chop the mushrooms and add to the pan. Fry for 20 minutes on low heat while adding tiny bit of water if needed, add finely chopped spinach leaves and fry for another 5 minutes. Meanwhile boil your sweet potato and mush with little bit of olive oil. Combine mushrooms, mushed sweet potato and buckwheat flour. Form the patties and fry them in olive oil until ready on both sides. Makes 5 patties.

Per serving: 111 calories, sodium 10 mg, potassium 228 mg, sugars 1 g

18. Corn chowder with white beans and cauliflower

Benefits: Corn is a rich source of many vitamins and minerals. By eating fiber-rich white beans you can lower your risks of having cancer and high blood pressure.

Ingredients:

- 100 g sweet corn
- 50 g white beans
- 2 small potatoes
- 100 g cauliflower
- 50 ml low fat milk
- 1 medium onion

How to prepare: Peel, roughly chop and boil the potatoes until ready. Add milk and let cool down. Meanwhile fry your chopped onion in olive oil with crumbled cauliflower for about 15 minutes until golden brown. In a saucepan combine the potatoes with liquid, cauliflower, add cooked beans and sweet corn. Serve warm. Add a little bit of low fat cheese on top (optional). Makes 3 servings.

Per serving: 191 calories, sodium 29 mg, potassium 1018 mg, sugars 5.9 g

19. Grilled watermelon with pomegranate, feta cheese and orange

Benefits: Watermelon is a significant lsource of vitamins A, B6 and C, antioxidants, amino acids and potassium. Feta cheese supplies key vitamins and minerals for your diet.

Ingredients:

- 100 g watermelon
- 70 g feta cheese
- 1 medium pomegranate
- 0.5 medium orange

How to prepare: Chop your watermelon (dont forget to take away the seeds), place it onto the cooking tray and set your oven to grill mode (alternatively use a normal grill oven), cook the watermelon until it is slightly tender on the sides. Cut feta cheese into cubes and combine with diced orange and pomegranate. Add grilled watermelon and serve as soon as possible. Makes 2 servings.

Per serving: 157 calories, sodium 391 mg, potassium 277 mg, sugars 15 g

20. Russian diet cabbage soup

Benefits: Potatoes are very high in potassium and if eaten in moderation will only have positive impact on your health. This soup is extremely low fat and will help you lose all those extra pounds and boost your metabolism.

Ingredients:

- 100 g cabbage
- 100 g carrots
- 1 medium onion
- 2 small potatoes
- paesley and dill (to taste)

How to prepare: Combine grated carrots and chopped onion together on a frying pan and fry for 10 minutes until golden brown. Meanwhile cut the cabbage and potatoes into medium piecesof same size and start boiling them. Halfway through (after about 15 minutes) add the carrots and leave the soup to simmer on medium heat for another 15-20 minutes. Add chopped parsley and dill. Makes 3 servings.

Per serving: 101 calories, sodium 14 mg, potassium 571 mg, sugars 4 g

21. Sweet potato carrot pumpkin soup with cumin and coriander

Benefits: This soup is packed with potassium and other blood pressure lowering minerals.

Ingredients:

- 1 medium sweet potato
- 2 carrots
- 100 g pumpkin
- 1 medium red onion
- 100 ml low fat milk (preferably almond milk)
- cumin (to taste)
- coriander (to taste)

Shred sweet potato, carrots and pumpkin into a bowl and mix well. In a saucepan heat 1 tbsp of olive oil and fry the chopped onion until tender. Add a little bit of olive oil and combine with the shredded vegetables, all cumin and coriander to taste and mix well. Pour milk into the saucepan slowly while stirring and leave on a low heat for 30 minutes. Turn off the heat and let cool. Using blender create a smooth creamy consistency. Serve warm, add pumpkin seeds or shredded coconut on top (optional).

Makes 2 servings.

Per serving: 197 calories, sodium 90 mg, potassium 726 mg, sugars 12 g

22. Cauliflower crust pumpkin pizza

Benefits: Cauliflower is a good source of vitamin C, protein, thiamin, riboflavin, niacin, magnesium, phosphorus, fiber, vitamin B6, folate, pantothenic acid, potassium, and manganese. Enjoy your pizza without having to worry about gaining weight.

Ingredients:

- 100 g cauliflower
- 1 large red onions
- 50 g pumpkin
- 50 g tomato puree
- basil (to taste)
- 40 g buckwheat flour
- 1 small egg
- 40 g low fat cheese or mozzarella

How to prepare:

Boil cauliflower for 5 minutes on medium heat and put in a blender. Drain well and spread on a towel until it dries. Beat one egg and combine with the cauliflower and buckwheat flour, knead for a while and spread on a parchment paper. Cook the sauce: mix shredded pumpkin with pureed tomatoes and chopped onion and simmer for 15 minutes until relatively thick. Add basil (optional). Spread sauce over the crust, add shredded low fat cheese or mozzarella on top and bake for 30 minutes at 425 F.

Per whole pizza: 377 calories, sodium 354 mg, potassium 1151 mg, sugars 14 g

23. Light beet and orange salad

Benefits: Beets are high in immune-boosting vitamin C, fiber, and essential minerals like potassium and manganese. Oranges are an excellent source of vitamin C, dietary fiber, vitamin A, calcium, copper and potassium.

Ingredients:

- 1 medium beet
- 1 medium orange
- 40 g pine nuts
- spinach
- 30 g low fat yogurt

How to prepare: Boil the beets and cut into cubes, dice the oranges. Mix all the ingredients together. Drizzle with yogurt and serve. Makes 3 servings.

Per serving: 143 calories, sodium 43 mg, potassium 390 mg, sugars 8 g

24. Mashed potatoes with light mushrooms sauce

Benefits: Mushrooms are also good sources of selenium, an antioxidant mineral, as well as copper, niacin, potassium and phosphorous. Additionally, mushrooms provide protein, vitamin C and iron. **Combined with mashed potatoes they create classic creamy flavor.**

Ingredients:

- 2 medium potatoes
- 100 g mushrooms
- 100g low fat yogurt
- 30 g low fat cheese

How to prepare: Wash the potatoes thoroughly but don't peel it. Bake for 30 minutes or until tender at 400 F. Meanwhile roughly chop the mushrooms and fry in olive oil for 20 minutes. Let the potatoes cool, cut in half lengthwise and take away the contents. Mush it and combine with yogurt and mushrooms. Stuff the potatoes again, put shredded cheese on top and bake for another 5 minutes. Makes 2 servings.

Per serving: 143 calories, sodium 43 mg, potassium 390 mg, sugars 8 g

25. Mushroom and carrot pot pie

Benefits: This recipe is an awesome alternative to fat-packed usual pot pie, though doesn't lack in taste and remains to be an awesome example of comfort food.

Ingredients:

- 100 g mushrooms
- 100g carrots
- 50 g potatoes
- 40 g low fat yogurt
- 30 g low fat cheese
- 1 medium red onion

How to prepare: Combine shredded carrots, chopped mushrooms and onion on a pan and fry them for 20 minutes on low heat while adding water if necessary. Meanwhile boil the potatoes and mush them with yogurt. Put mushrooms to the bottom of a baking form, then cover with mushed potatoes and add shredded cheese on top. Bake for 30 minutes at 400 F. Makes 2 servings.

Per serving: 98calories, sodium 113 mg, potassium 511 mg, sugars 6 g

26. Avocado carrot and orange salad with spinach and feta cheese

Benefits: This recipe combines all the best foods to lower your blood pressure and is very beneficial for your digestive health and heart.

Ingredients:

- 1 ripe avocado
- 100g carrots
- 100 g orange
- spinach
- 100 g feta cheese
- 1 tbsp honey

How to prepare: Cut carrots into rings, drizzle with honey and fry in olive oil until slightly golden. Cut avocado, oranges and feta cheese into cubes. Combine all the ingredients and serve. Makes 3 servings.

Per serving: 260 calories, sodium 399 mg, potassium 456 mg, sugars 9 g

27. Stuffed cabbage leaves

Benefits: Black rice, a super-food that is gaining popularity these days, is very beneficial for your immune health and is low in calorie alternative to usual rice. Raisins are an awesome source of B vitamins, iron and potassium.

Ingredients:

- 3 medium whole cabbage leaves
- 100 g black rice
- 100 g basmati rice
- 50 g raisins
- curry powder (to taste)
- tumeric (to taste)

How to prepare: Boil cabbage leaves until tender. Meanwhile cook both types of rice according to the packaging. Add curry powder and tumeric, combine with the raisins and put the mixture inside each cabbage leaf. Serve warm. Makes 3 servings.

Per serving: 230 calories, sodium 9 mg, potassium 227 mg, sugars 10 g

28. Quinoa primavera

Benefits: A great alternative to a traditional spanish pasta primavera is packed with healthy nutrients, low in calories and high in protein.

Ingredients:

- 100 g quinoa
- 100 g broccoli
- 50 g peas
- 100 g cherry tomatoes
- 1 small carrot

How to prepare: Chop all the vegetables and put into a saucepan. Drizzle with olive oil and fry for 5 minutes. Thoroughly wash quinoa and put into the saucepan. Cover with water and boil until all the liquid is absorbed. Makes 3 servings.

Per serving: 160 calories, sodium 26 mg, potassium 466 mg, sugars 3 g

29. Aubergines baked in tomato sauce

Benefits: Aubergines are an excellent source of dietary fibre, vitamins B1 and B6, potassium and various minerals. Tomatoes are packed with vitamin C, biotin, molybdenum and vitamin K, copper, potassium, manganese, dietary fiber, vitamin A , vitamin B6, folate, niacin, vitamin E and phosphorus.

Ingredients:

- 1 medium aubergine
- 2 giant tomatoes
- 1 medium bell pepper
- 50 g olives
- 1 medium red onion
- 50 g mozzarella
- basil (to taste)
- rosemary (to taste)

How to prepare: Finely chop the onion and fry until golden brown, add chopped tomatoes, pepper, olives and spices. Simmer for 15 minutes on medium heat.
Meanwhile slice the aubergine and cover with cold salted water. Let sit until the sauce is ready. Lay aubergine to the

bottom of a baking form and cover with sauce. Put mozzarella on top and bake for 40 minutes at 400 F. Makes 3 servings.

Per serving: 140 calories, sodium 254 mg, potassium 380 mg, sugars 5 g

30. Baked beans

Benefits: Apples, carrots and tomatoes: three best foods for weight loss together. Kidney beans are an awesome source of fiber and are considered one of the best healthy foods.

Ingredients:

- 100 g apples
- 100 g carrots
- 1 can of red beans
- 100 g tomato puree
- rosemary (to taste)
- oregano (to taste)

How to prepare: Shred apples and carrots and mix together. Combine the shredded mix, tomato puree and beans. Add rosemary and oregano and bake for 20 minutes at 400 F. Makes 3 servings.

Per serving: 250 calories, sodium 40 mg, potassium 1122 mg, sugars 8 g

31. Curried cauliflower

Benefits: Curry, apart from having an unique flavor that goes with literally any vegetables, is also a greet immune health booster. Cauliflower is perfect for weight loss and digestive health improvement.

Ingredients:

- 200 g cauliflower
- curry (to taste)
- 2 tbsp lemon juice
- coriander (to taste)

How to prepare: Roughly chop or crumble cauliflower, drizzle with olive oil and lemon juice, add curry powder and coriander and bake for 20 minutes at 400 F. Makes 2 servings.

Per serving: 110 calories, sodium 33 mg, potassium 380 mg, sugars 2 g

32. Beans and zucchini patties

Benefits: Zucchini has a high content of vitamin A, **magnesium**, **folate**, **potassium**, copper, and **protein**. Buckwheat flour is a great substitution of wheat flour, it's low in calories and also beneficial for your health.

Ingredients:

- 1 medium zucchini
- 1 can black beans
- 1 medium red onion
- chilli (to taste)
- cumin (to taste)
- 50 g buckwheat flour

How to prepare: Roughly chop the onion and fry in olive oil until golden brown, add chilli powder and cumin. Shred zucchini and put in a blender with beans and onion. Blend well, add flour and form patties. Fry on both sides until crispy. Makes 6 patties.

Per serving: 151 calories, sodium 7 mg, potassium 460 mg, sugars 2 g

33. Baked potatoes with polenta and rosemary

Benefits: Polenta is a low carbohydrate food rich in vitamin A and C, it also has benefits like cancer and heart disease prevention.

Ingredients:

- 4 small potatoes
- 50 g polenta
- rosemary
- 50 g low fat yogurt

How to prepare: Wash potatoes thoroughly and peel. Make a coating: Mix polenta with yogurt and rosemary. Cover potatoes with the coating and bake for 30 minutes at 400 F. makes 4 servings.

Per serving: 89 calories, sodium 12 mg, potassium 233 mg, sugars 1.5 g

34. Sweet potato, beans and avocado salad

Benefits: This recipe is the best option if you're looking for something packed with protein and fiber.

Ingredients:

- 1 medium sweet potato
- 1 ripe avocado
- 1can black beans
- 1 tbsp lemon juice
- coriander
- parsley

How to prepare: Peel sweet potato and cut into cubes. Bake until tender. Meanwhile combine mushed avocado, beans, coriander and parsley. Add sweet potato, mix well. Drizzle with lemon juice and serve slightly warm. Makes 3 servings.

Per serving: 172 calories, sodium 19 mg, potassium 512 mg, sugars 3 g

35. Spicy carrot rice

Benefits: This low fat recipe is the best option to impress your relatives and friends. Cashews add a whole lot of benefits to it: they are packed with copper, manganese, magnesium, phosphorus, iron, selenium, vitamin B6.

Ingredients:

- 100 g brown rice or black rice
- 2 small carrots
- 1 medium red onion
- 1 medium tomato
- 30 g cashews
- cinnamon
- coriander

How to prepare: Chop the onion, tomato, shred the carrots, add cinnamon and coriander and fry for 15 minutes on low heat. Meanwhile cook your rice as stated on the packaging. Combine vegetable sauce, rice and crumbled cashews. Serve immediately. Makes 4 servings.

Per serving: 160 calories, sodium 22 mg, potassium 302 mg, sugars 3 g

36. Pineapple, corn and curry quinoa

Benefits: Pineapple is an awesome source of potassium, copper, manganese, calcium, magnesium, vitamin C, beta carotene, thiamin, B6, and folate. Corn will surely become your favorite sweet foods of your new healthy diet.

Ingredients:

- 80 g quinoa
- 100 g pineapple
- 1 can sweet corn
- curry powder

How to prepare: Cook the quinoa according to the packaging. Chop your pineapple, add corn and curry powder. Combine your mixture with cooked quinoa and serve cold. Makes 3 servings.

Per serving: 156 calories, sodium 2 mg, potassium 306 mg, sugars 5 g

37. Baked zucchini with mushrooms and pine nuts

Benefits: Pine nuts contain nutrients that help boost energy, are also a good source of magnesium.

Ingredients:

- 1 medium zucchini
- 100 g mushrooms
- 40 g pine nuts
- 2 tbsp olive oil
- 1 tbsp garlic powder

How to prepare: Cut zucchini into rings, dice the onions, add garlic powder and pine nuts. Drizzle with olive oil and bake for 30 minutes at 375 F. Makes 3 servings.

Per serving: 197 calories, sodium 9 mg, potassium 388 mg, sugars 3 g

38. Sweet potato pudding with mixed nuts

Benefits: Sweet potato is high in protein and an awesome taste that goes well in both sweet and savory recipes. Nuts are packed with potassium and magnesium, essential minerals to lower your high blood pressure.

Ingredients:

- 1 medium sweet potato
- 1 cup coconut milk or low fat milk
- 1 tbsp. honey
- 50 g mixed nuts (walnuts, pistachios, hazelnuts etc.)

How to prepare: Boil sweet potato and put in a blender, pour in coconut milk, and honey. Add mixed nuts and blend well. Distribute the mixture between 3 separate cups and leave in a freezer overnight.

Per serving: 208 calories, sodium 162 mg, potassium 416 mg, sugars 12 g

39. Spring onion buckwheat flat cakes

Benefits: Spring onion is high in Vitamin C, Vitamin B2, thiamine, Vitamin A, Vitamin K, copper, phosphorous, magnesium, potassium, chromium, manganese and fiber. They boost the immunity and help prevent multiple illnesses like heart disease.

Ingredients:

- 30 g spring onion
- 50 g buckwheat flour
- 1 egg
- coriander
- parsley
- dill

How to prepare: Finely chop the spring onion, combine with coriander, parsley and sill. Mix 1 egg with the buckwheat flour and onion. Fry on both sides. Makes 4 small flat cakes.

Per serving: 60 calories, sodium 18 mg, potassium 108 mg, sugars 0.6 g

40. Risotto with cherries, cranberries and coconut

Benefits: Cherries contain fiber, vitamin C, carotenoids, they help prevent cancer or stroke and are also very good for weight loss. Cranberries are a very good source of vitamin C, dietary fiber, manganese, vitamin E, vitamin K, copper and pantothenic acid.

Ingredients:

- 100 g rice
- 100 ml low fat milk or coconut milk
- 50 g cherries
- 30 g candied cranberries
- shredded coconut (to taste)
- almond flakes (optional)
- 2 tbsp honey

How to prepare: Bring milk to a boil and add rice while stirring constantly. Cook the rice on low heat until the mixture resembles rice porridge. Add your berries and honey. Mix well. Sprinkle with shredded coconut and almond flakes. Makes 3 servings.

Per serving: 198 calories, sodium 20 mg, potassium 115 mg, sugars 14 g

41. Apples and celery soup

Benefits: Celery is very rich in vitamin K, folate, vitamin A, potassium, vitamin C and dietary fiber. This juice and light soup is low in calories and fat.

Ingredients:

- 100 g celery
- 2 medium apples
- 100 ml vegetable stock
- 1 medium onion
- 2 tbsp olive oil

How to prepare: Heat 2 tbsp olive oil in a medium saucepan, add finely chopped onion and fry until golden brown. Add shredded apple and celery. Pour in vegetable stock and 50 ml water. Cook on low heat for 30 minutes. Makes 3 servings.

Per serving: 163 calories, sodium 29 mg, potassium 270 mg, sugars 15 g

42. Beetroot carrot soup

Benefits: Beetroots can improve digestion and lower blood pressure. This soup is packed with affordable basic vegetables that go amazing together and are essential for weight loss.

Ingredients:

- 1 medium beetroot
- 2 medium carrots
- 1 giant potato
- 100 ml vegetable stock
- 1 small zucchini
- 1 medium tomato

Ingredients: Wash thoroughly and peel beetroot, carrots, zucchini and potatoes. Add chopped tomatoes and cover with vegetable stock and 200 ml water. Bring to a boil and simmer for 40 minutes on low heat. Serve warm. Makes 4 servings.

Per serving: 74 calories, sodium 61 mg, potassium 556 mg, sugars 7 g

43. Buckwheat shakshuka

Benefits: Buckwheat and tomato sauce go incredibly well together and create unique flavour of this middle eastern dish.

Ingredients:

- 150 g tomato puree
- 2 small eggs
- 50 g buckwheat
- 1 medium red onion
- parsley
- dill
- cumin
- paprika

How to prepare: Roughly chop the onion and fry in olive oil until golden brown, add tomato puree and leave to simmer on low heat for 10 minutes, gradually adding your spices. Crack 2 eggs into the sauce and don't stir. Cover with a lid and leave on the stove until eggs are ready. Meanwhile cook your buckwheat in slightly salted water according to the packaging. Serve two dishes alongside. Makes 2 servings.

Per serving:103 calories, sodium 75 mg, potassium 459 mg, sugars 6 g

44. Summer vegetables bake

Bell peppers as well as cherry tomatoes are packed with healthy nutrients, they have anti-cancer and blood pressure lowering properties.

Ingredients:

- 100 g cherry tomatoes
- 100 g yellow cherry tomatoes
- 2 medium red onions
- 1 small yellow bell pepper

How to prepare: Cut onions into large pieces, chop the pepper and half cherry tomatoes. Combine together and drizzle with olive oil. Bake for 30 minutes at 400 F. Makes 3 servings.

Per serving: 49 calories, sodium 7 mg, potassium 317 mg, sugars 6 g

45. Spinach broccoli lentils

Benefits: Combining the two ultimate greens (broccoli and spinach) with lentils is surely a good choice. Lentils are an excellent source of molybdenum, folate, dietary fiber, copper, phosphorus, manganese, iron, protein, vitamin B1, pantothenic acid, zinc, potassium and vitamin B6.

Ingredients:

- 100 g broccoli
- fresh spinach leaves
- 50 g red lentils
- 30 g low fat cheese

How to prepare: Chop spinach leaves, broccoli, add lentils. Put mixture into a saucepan, cover with water. Cook on low heat until all the liquid is incorporated and lentils are ready. Sprinkle with grated low fat cheese. Makes 2 servings.

Per serving: 132 calories, sodium 114 mg, potassium 435 mg, sugars 1 g

46. Pistachios and avocado pesto

Benefits: Pistachios contain nutrients such as carbohydrates,proteins, fats, dietary fiber, phosphorus, potassium, thiamine, vitamin B-6, beta-carotene, calcium,iron, magnesium etc. This pesto can surely be called best healthy protein source.

Ingredients:

- 1 ripe avocado
- 30 g basil leaves
- 40 g pistachios
- 2 tbsp olive oil

How to prepare: Blend all the ingredients together. Sevre alongside mushed potatoes or on toast.

Total (300 g) : 870 calories, sodium 277 mg, potassium 1477 mg, sugars 4 g

47. Summer fruit salad

Benefits: Apples, melons, blueberries and kiwis are all amazing sources of potassium and other essential healthy nutrients.

Ingredients:

- 3 medium apples
- 100 g blueberries
- 2 ripe kiwis
- 150 g melon

How to prepare: Chop all the ingredients and mix together. Makes 5 servings.

Per serving: 97 calories, sodium 7 mg, potassium 307 mg, sugars 18 g

48. Buckwheat and lentils granola

Benefits: Instead of using sugar packed granola from your local store prepare this simple healthy breakfast granola by yourself. It doesn't lack in flavor though is so much more beneficial to your health.

Ingredients:

- 50 g buckwheat
- 50 g red lentils
- 30 g shredded coconut
- 100 g mixed nuts
- 200 ml low fat milk (or almond milk)

How to prepare: Cook the buckwheat and lentils according to the packaging. Mix them together and spread on a parchment paper in an even layer. Bake for 30 minutes at 400 F. Add nuts andcoconut. Pour in milk and serve. Makes 4 servings.

Per serving: 246 calories, sodium 101 mg, potassium 359 mg, sugars 5 g

ADDITIONAL TITLES FROM THIS AUTHOR

70 Effective Meal Recipes to Prevent and Solve Being Overweight: Burn Fat Fast by Using Proper Dieting and Smart Nutrition

By

Joe Correa CSN

48 Acne Solving Meal Recipes: The Fast and Natural Path to Fixing Your Acne Problems in Less Than 10 Days!

By

Joe Correa CSN

41 Alzheimer's Preventing Meal Recipes: Reduce or Eliminate Your Alzheimer's Condition in 30 Days or Less!

By

Joe Correa CSN

70 Effective Breast Cancer Meal Recipes: Prevent and Fight Breast Cancer with Smart Nutrition and Powerful Foods

By

Joe Correa CSN

www.ingramcontent.com/pod-product-compliance
Lightning Source LLC
Chambersburg PA
CBHW052124070526
44586CB00016B/2080